CHRISTINA AGUILERA
backstage pass

By Jan Gabriel

SCHOLASTIC INC.

New York   Toronto   London   Auckland   Sydney   Mexico City   New Delhi   Hong Kong

Photography Credits:

Front Cover: Bernhard Kuhmstedt/Retna; Back Cover: Bernhard Kuhmstedt/Retna; Page 3: Ilpo Musto/London Features; Page 4: Walter McBride/Retna; Page 5: (left) Tara Canova/Retna; Page 5: (right) Jen Lowery/London Features; Page 6: Ilpo Musto/London Features; Page 7: Tara Canova/Retna; Page 8: (left) Walter McBride/Retna; Page 8: (right) Tara Canova/Retna; Page 9: Reggie Casagrande/Corbis Outline; Page 10: Sean Murphy/Retna; Page 11: (left) Ron Wolfson/London Features; Page 11: (right) Jon James/London Features; Page 12: (left) George DeSota/London Features; Page 12: (right) Gary Gershoff/ Retna; Page 13: Steve Granitz/Retna; Page 14: Everett Collection; Page 15: (left) Reggie Casagrande/Corbis Outline; Page 15: (right) Ilpo Musto/London Features; Page16: (left) Ilpo Musto/London Features; Page 16: (right) Steve Granitz/Retna; Page 17: Dennis Van Tine/London Features; Page18: Walter McBride/Retna; Page 19: (left) Lawrence Marano/London Features; Page 19: (right) Gerardo Somoza/Corbis Outline; Page 20: JG/All Action Retna; Page 21: Barry Talesnick/Retna; Page 22: (left) Steve Granitz/Retna; Page 22: (right) Steve Granitz/Retna; Page 23: (left) Steve Granitz/Retna; Page 23: (right) Barry Talesnick/Retna; Page 24: (top) Tara Canova/Retna/top; Page 24: (bottom) Walter McBride/Retna; Page 25: (left) Steve Granitz/Retna/left; Page 25: (right) Steve Sands/Corbis Outline; Page 26: (left) Jeff Slocomb/Corbis Outline; Page 26: (right) Armando Gallo/Retna; Page 27: Barry Talesnick/Retna; Page 28: Sean Murphy/Retna; Page 29: (left) Dennis Van Tine/London Features; Page 29: (right) Ilpo Musto/London Features; Page 30: Scott Weiner/Retna; Page 31: Tara Canova/Retna; Page 32: (left) Ilpo Musto/London Features; Page 32: (right) Sean Murphy/Retna; Page 33: Reggie Casagrande/Corbis Outline; Page 34: JG/All Action Retna; Page 35: (left) Tara Canova/Retna; Page 35: (right) JG/All Action Retna; Page 36: (left) JG/All Action Retna; Page 36: (right) Jen Lowery/London Features; Page 37: (left) Steve Granitz/Retna; Page 37: (right) Tara Canova/Retna; Page 38: Bernhard Kuhmstedt/Retna; Page 38: (bottom inset) Steve Granitz/Retna; Page 39: Paul Smith/Feature Flash Retna; Page 40: Ron Wolfson/London Features; Page 41: Steve Granitz/Retna; Page 42: Steve Granitz/Retna; Page 43: (left) Barry Talesnick/Retna; Page 43: (right) Armando Gallo/Retna; Page 44: Leo Sorel/Retna; Page 45: Reggie Casagrande/Corbis Outline; Page 45: (bottom inset) Ron Wolfson/London Features; Page 46: Steve Granitz/Retna; Page 47: Walter McBride/Retna; Page 48: Armando Gallo/Retna

ISBN 0-439-14002-1

Design by Peter Koblish

12 11 10 9 8 7 6 5 4 3 2 1   0 1 2 3 4 5 6/0

Printed in the U.S.A.
First Scholastic printing, July 2000

GUIDE TO WHAT'S INSIDE

The little girl with the big voice is a huge star!

3

★INTRODUCTION★
MAKE A WISH ✦

When Christina Aguilera was little, she made a wish. She knew, from the get-go, what this girl wanted, what this girl needed, what exactly would make her happy.

She hoped to be a singer, a performer, a star.

Now that she's (mostly) all grown up, that wish has come true. And has it made her happy?

Duh!!

For by the time she blew out the candles on her nineteenth birthday, Christina Aguilera had achieved bigtime stardom. Today, she is an official pop princess who has it all: an amazingly powerful voice, mesmerizing stage presence, a string of hit songs, and major awardage. Her talent has been totally recognized, too. *Time* magazine even called her, "One of the most strikingly gifted singers to come along since Mariah Carey."

Cool!

Okay, here come the stats: Her first CD, *Christina Aguilera*, hit number one — the very week it came out. It ranked as

"Society has created this image of the perfect girl. Lots of times we buy into that, to the point where we don't feel good about ourselves. It's my mission to change that whole mind-set."

the ninth top-selling album for all of 1999, having sold 3.43 million copies during that year (it's now doubled that figure).

Her singles, "Genie in a Bottle," "What a Girl Wants," and "I Turn to You" all sat snugly in the number one spot in the pop charts for weeks on end.

Video votes on *TRL*, cover stories in all the teen magazines, Grammy nominations (and a win for Best New Artist) — it's all "business as usual" on Planet Christina these days.

But it didn't take a "genie in a bottle" to make it happen. That, as everyone knows, is make-believe, a fantasy. Instead, it took a whole lot of wanting, waiting, and most of all working. That's the reality. And this: choking back the tears sometimes, burying the hurt, relying on a whole lot of support, and a little bit of luck.

A pair of mouse ears didn't hurt either. More about that later!

So settle in and read all about it. Here's the tale of how a tiny girl with a huge voice and huger dream popped — not out of a bottle, but from the suburbs of Pittsburgh, PA — to become one of today's top selling and best-loved teen singers. Here comes Christina's story, her stats and facts, her vision, her music, and her message to fans.

"I grew up watching the Grammys and wanted to be there — the Best New Artist was my dream."

Christina was voted "Most Kissable" by on-line fans, beating out Britney, Shania, and Mariah!

CHRISTINA AGUILERA

CHAPTER ONE
BABY STEPS

"I've always felt a need to be in the spotlight."

Most people take years figuring out what they want to do with their lives. The lucky ones eventually find something they love and get to do it. It's the rare person who just "knows" what she or he was meant to do — and have the talent and the luck to fulfill that destiny.

Meet Christina Aguilera.

From the time she could talk, she could sing. From the time she could walk, she could dance. From the time she could smile, she could light up a room. She's a born entertainer.

Christina's story starts in the borough of New York City called Staten Island. She was the first child of Shelly, an Irish-American musician, and Fausto Aguilera, who comes from the South American country of Ecuador. The couple had met at college and married soon after. Though English was the dominant language at home, Spanish was spoken as well, and to this day, Christina can understand it. Although Shelly was a talented violinist and pianist,

she earned her living as a Spanish translator. Fausto was a career military man who eventually rose to the rank of U.S. Army Sergeant. Both parents

"One thing I've always wanted to do is sing with a rock band — I really want to rock out and be the girl lead in a male group, like Gwen in No Doubt."

the bed and serenade them. A few years later, she'd open the window of the family apartment and sing to passersby on the street.

She'd warble into a shampoo bottle in the bathtub. Or, "I would take a twirling baton and use it as my 'ickaphone' because I couldn't pronounce microphone," Christina giggles, adding, "I'd lay a towel on the floor as my stage."

All during her toddler years, the family traveled. Her dad's military career took them from their Staten Island home base, to houses in Texas, New Jersey, and even Japan.

The year Christina turned five, her world went topsy turvy.

doted on their baby daughter, who was born on December 18, 1980.

And both knew she was something special.

How could they not?

The little girl always had a song in her heart, and on her lips. And she liked having an audience. "I wanted to perform as long as I could remember — since I've been in diapers!" Christina told reporters.

At the age of two, she would line her stuffed animals up on

Mom, Shelly, is Christina's best friend.

On the serendipitous side: that was the year she first saw the video of the movie, *The Sound of Music.*

It would change everything.

"The Little Girl With the Big Voice"

Christina says, "At age five I was really connecting with music as something special to me. I remember being that age when I saw *The Sound of Music* and I used to sing all the songs. I would sing at friends' parties. And when people started applauding and cheering for me, I realized that this was what I wanted to do for a career."

While her mom knew Christina was a prodigy, "It was probably my grandmother who really noticed there was something there," Christina explained to Scholastic. Certainly, both helped her take the "baby" steps toward her dream.

They started with block parties, where Christina would entertain. She had an entire repertoire of songs — some from that movie musical, others from copying the radio. Everyone loved her.

"I was signing autographs when I didn't know how to write cursive. I would be sitting there printing, when I barely knew how to spell my name." It became a routine she loved. "If there wasn't a block party or somewhere for her to sing, she'd

Some kids at school thought Christina was a snob — but she really wasn't at all.

On the upside, her little sister Rachel was born and, from the start, the two bonded. They're mega-close today.

On the downside, her parents split up. While her dad stayed in the Army, her mom moved the girls to Rochester, a suburb of Pittsburgh, PA, where they bunked with Christina's maternal grandma, Delcie Fidler.

At home in Pennsylvania, Christina still has chores to do — like baby-sitting her brother.

her town and at school. Christina well remembers her first grade performance of Whitney Houston's "I Wanna Dance With Somebody." She was all of seven years old.

But music wasn't just something she did for applause. She did it all the time, whether there was an audience or not. Sometimes, she preferred it to socializing. "Kids used to come over and ask if I could play — and my mom would tell them I was playing — singing all by myself," she confessed to *Seventeen Online*, adding, "I guess I was weird."

On the homefront, things were looking up. Her mom had remarried, and paramedic James Kearns became Christina and Rachel's stepdad. Instantly, the family expanded to include James' daughter Stephanie and his son Casey. Eventually, Shelly and James had a child of their own, the now four-year-old Robert Michael.

Christina's musical influences began to expand, too. She listened to everything — from pop, to soul, and hip-hop, even blues and jazz music, spinning disks by such legends as Etta James, Billie Holliday, and B.B. King.

Whitney Houston, with whom she is

get irritable," her mom confessed to *Rolling Stone* magazine.

Soon she was performing at community events, and entering talent shows in often compared, was her original idol. "I adored Whitney," she told *YM* magazine. "I just really felt that whole soul thing. And she is such a chameleon, always reinventing herself. I look up to her for that."

As singing took over more of her life, Christina earned a fond nickname. "The little girl with the big voice," is what local newspapers called her. Because she was so small physically, one reporter dubbed her, a "Micro-Diva."

Soon, she was being called on to perform at professional

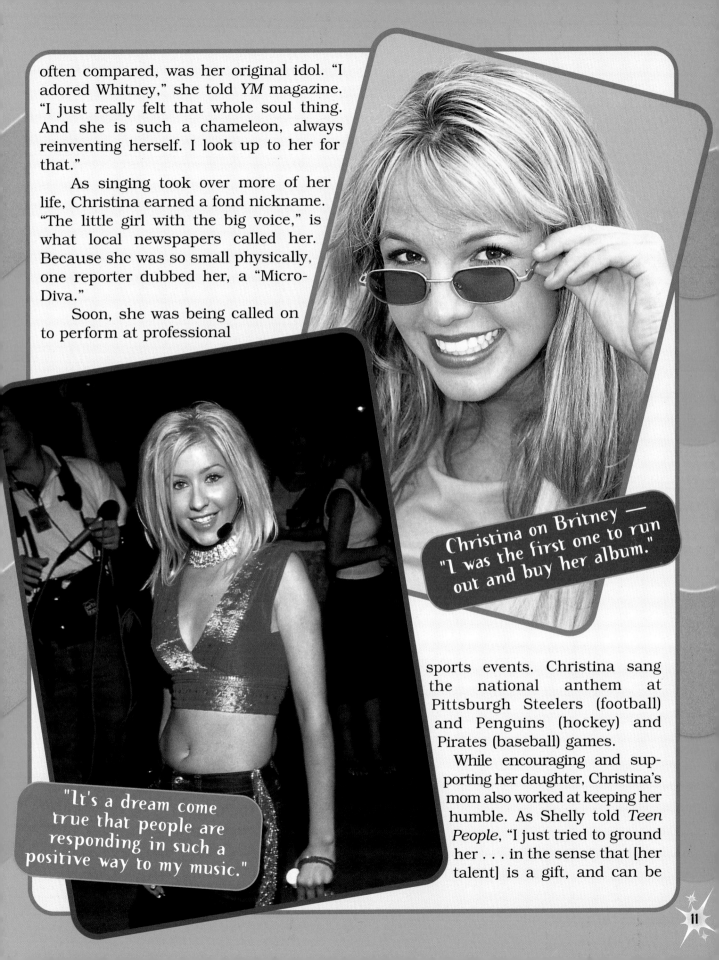

Christina on Britney — "I was the first one to run out and buy her album."

"It's a dream come true that people are responding in such a positive way to my music."

sports events. Christina sang the national anthem at Pittsburgh Steelers (football) and Penguins (hockey) and Pirates (baseball) games.

While encouraging and supporting her daughter, Christina's mom also worked at keeping her humble. As Shelly told *Teen People*, "I just tried to ground her . . . in the sense that [her talent] is a gift, and can be taken away. I didn't want her to think, 'How great I am!' I've always told her, 'Your singing is nice, but what makes me proud of you is the kind of person you are."

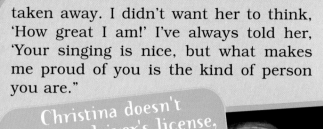

Christina doesn't have her driver's license, but she wouldn't mind a cute little sports car!

"I Was a Star Search Loser"

The TV show *Star Search* used to be one of Christina's favorites. She'd watch as young unknowns would sing, dance, act — whatever their talent was — in hopes of catching a big break, the one that would lead to stardom. In Christina's heart, that dream burned brightly.

For the most part, *Star Search* was taped in Los Angeles — no way could a little girl from Pittsburgh get there. Then one day, *Star Search* came to her. She was eight years old and won a spot to compete on the show from an open audition held locally. When she got on the show,

"It's hard to make friends when you do what I do — I travel a lot."

she did her rendition of Whitney Houston's "The Greatest Love of All."

Christina put her heart and soul into that performance, and she was amazing — but not enough to win. A twelve-year-old boy sang the rock 'n' roll antique, "Hey There Lonely Girl," and he took home the top prize. Christina was a good sport about it — she had to be!

"My mom made me go back out and shake his hand and tell him I was happy he won," she confessed in *Rolling Stone* magazine. "Tears were running down my face. Awful!" Little could she know that that loss would lead to another audition. And that one would propel her toward her destiny.

She admits to crushing on Enrique Iglesias: "He's sooo good-looking and a really excellent artist."

☀CHAPTER TWO☀
THE NEW MICKEY MOUSE CLUB

That's Christina in the middle row on the right. "Little Brit-Brit" is just below.

"I loved being around kids who had the same passions I did."

In 1990, Christina was nine years old. One of her favorite TV shows aired on the Disney Channel. It was called *The New Mickey Mouse Club* — or, *MMC*, for short. The show starred a troupe of talented 'tweens and teens, who'd sing, dance, act, and do comedy routines. None were big stars at the time, each had gotten on by auditioning — tryouts that were open to any kid in the country.

That year, open auditions for *MMC* were held in Pittsburgh, PA, right outside Christina's hometown. Five hundred kids came to try out, among 'em, that little local star with the big voice, Christina Aguilera.

The director of the show, Matt Casella, had an amazing eye for talent, and he remembers Christina well. "She was like a Whitney Houston," he told *People* magazine. "A triple threat, able to sing, dance, and act."

So he snapped her up to be on the show right then and there? Nuh-uh! He rejected her!

But not because there were other kids at the audition who were better: there were other kids who were older. Christina was turned away that year for being too young. But she wasn't forgotten.

In 1992, when the show was in its sixth season, Christina got the call to join up. It meant spending her summer in Orlando, Florida, away from friends and family. She didn't hesitate for one second. And has never regretted it.

Christina jumped right in to her Mouseketeer role. During her two

"In a relationship, a girl wants respect, sincerity, and absolutely no game playing."

She learned to dance on *The New Mickey Mouse Club* show.

years as a regular, she sang lead on such songs as "Real Love," and "Love Can Move Mountains." On those two, she had several backup singers — among 'em, a curly-haired boy named Justin, and two girls. One, Keri, was several years older, and the other, who Christina came to call "Little Brit-Brit" was a year her junior.

As any pop and TV fan knows, those singers grew up to be 'N Sync's Justin Timberlake, Felicity's Keri Russell, and of all the other talented Mouseketeers (including, of course, 'N Sync's JC Chasez) was the best experience of Christina's life up to that point. "I got the most incredible education," she gushed to *Billboard* magazine, "both in terms of who I wanted to be as an artist, and in terms of how the business works. It gave me the focus I needed."

It also gave the naturally talented, but so far untrained, entertainer her first formal music lessons. "We had vocal

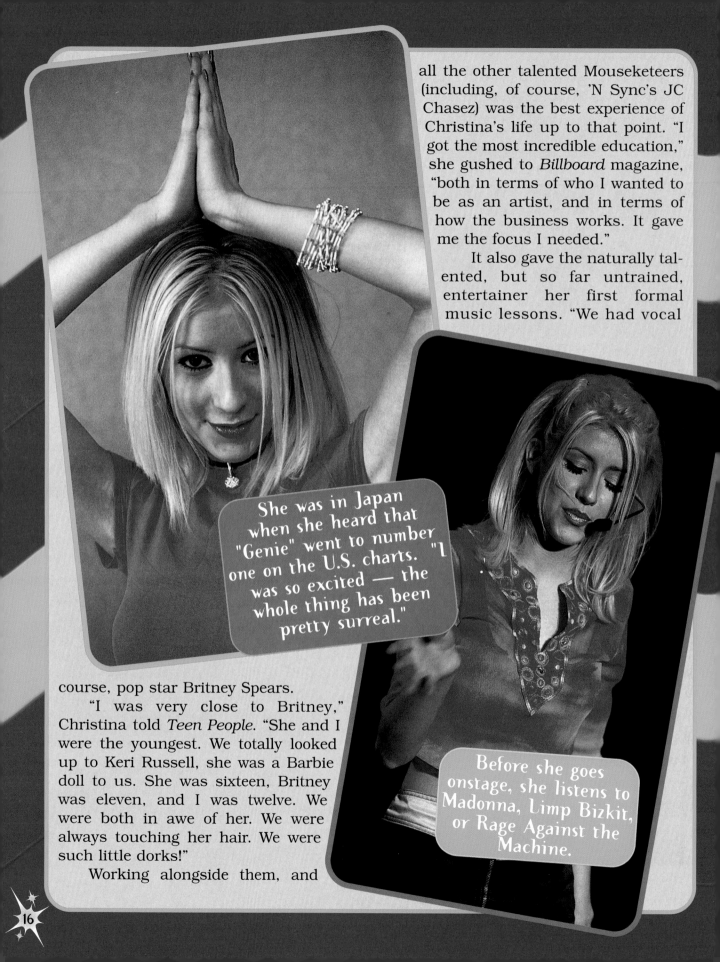

She was in Japan when she heard that "Genie" went to number one on the U.S. charts. "I was so excited — the whole thing has been pretty surreal."

Before she goes onstage, she listens to Madonna, Limp Bizkit, or Rage Against the Machine.

course, pop star Britney Spears.

"I was very close to Britney," Christina told *Teen People*. "She and I were the youngest. We totally looked up to Keri Russell, she was a Barbie doll to us. She was sixteen, Britney was eleven, and I was twelve. We were both in awe of her. We were always touching her hair. We were such little dorks!"

Working alongside them, and

coaches and choreographers, who helped me expand [on] my own instincts," Christina explained.

More important, maybe, for the first time in her life, she felt like she really fit in. For once, she wasn't considered weird because singing was her way of playing. "It was a great way to grow up. I loved being around kids who had the same passions I did."

It wasn't all work and no play on the Orlando soundstage. During breaks, the *MMC* group would hang out, play Ping-Pong, and goof off. The big joke, Christina said in *USA Today* was, "We used to tell each other that when the show ended, we'd all go off our separate ways and become stars. We're all so dedicated and driven, I'm not surprised at any of the success of my co-Mouseketeers."

She co-wrote the song "We're a Miracle," which is on the soundtrack of *Pokémon: The First Movie.*

★ CHAPTER THREE ★
SO YOU'RE A SUPERSTAR? ★
THAT DON'T IMPRESS ME MUCH!

Being a guest deejay is fun — hosting *TRL* was the coolest.

"*The roughest road often leads to the top.*"

Back when Christina was part of *The New Mickey Mouse Club*, she contributed to *MMC*'s Mini Magazine. Aside from dishing about her (then) likes and dislikes, she was also asked to share her favorite quote. The one she opted for, "The roughest road often leads to the top," might very well have come from experience.

The tough times began right after her *Star Search* appearance — and the tough times were all about jealousy. "As soon as *Star Search* happened, a lot of my mom's old friends, other parents, wouldn't talk to us anymore," she told *Teen People*. And then, the tires of her mom's car were slashed by (she believes) jealous parents.

As Christina's rep for being a local celeb spread, things got worse. Her mom divulged that she would cry every time her name got in the local paper because it meant more fear at school: threats not only of tire damage, but of getting beat up. She began having nightmares.

It wasn't just adult friends who dissed her family — it was teachers too. "Sometimes teachers made it difficult," she said in *Teen People*, "because I would be out with the flu, but they would assume it wasn't true. I would return to school and the teachers were like, 'Oh, she wasn't out sick; she was singing somewhere.'"

Sometimes, hair extensions can change her whole look!

Christina loves to eat potatoes — "Whether french fries, baked, mashed, scalloped, I eat three kinds every day," she told the *New York Post*.

"Singing Was an Outlet for Me. It Kept Me Going on My Toughest Days."

Harshest of all for any kid is not having friends. That's the sitch Christina found herself in for much of her elementary school years. Due to jealousy or whatever, her classmates often ignored her, making her feel like an outcast. Hard as that was, Christina

> "I really love belting out ballads . . . [that's] when you see the most personal, intimate side of Christina Aguilera."

would make one friend and then other girls would steal her away. It was tough," she confessed.

Between jealous parents, cruel kids, and teachers who didn't get it, things eventually got so bad that the family had to move so Christina could switch schools. Only that didn't help much. She felt just as much an outcast in her new school. The only solution seemed to be to leave school altogether, which she opted for, just after eighth grade. But Christina didn't ditch her education. Her mom, along with professional tutors, made sure she learned her lessons and kept her grades up.

In the end, dealing with "the harsh" toughened her up. As she described in *Teen People*, "[I had] to make a decision. [Was I] going to go down with the situation, or [would I] focus and succeed? My dream of becoming a recording artist kept me going."

is able to talk about it now.

"Going to a public school in a small town and not being around kids who did what I did made me feel like an outsider," she admitted to *Rolling Stone*. Worse was "grand theft friendship." "[Sometimes,] I

"The Note That Changed My Life"
All the time she was being tormented

in school, Christina's career continued its upward spiral. After *MMC* ended in 1996, she sang whenever and wherever she could, including gigs in Europe and Asia. Sometimes, she was the opening act for such megastars as Sheryl Crow and Diana Ross. Most notably, when she was sixteen, she recorded with Japanese singing sensation Keizo Nakanishi. Life on the road had its share of ups and downs, but Christina never lost sight of her goal: to snare a recording contract and make her own records. And always, always, to be a star.

Christina's big break came in 1998. That was the year artists were being recruited to sing on the soundtrack of the Disney animated feature, *Mulan.* They'd already lined up such stellar talent as Lea Salonga and Donny Osmond, but had one original song minus a singer. It was called "Reflection," and the challenge was to find a qualified female singer who could hit the note called "high E above middle C." The catch was the singer had to be young, since the song is about a teenager. Christina, of course, knew she could do it: she just had to find a way of

letting the album's producers know about her. Having a professional manager came in totally handy. He sent the record company a tape of her singing Whitney Houston's "I Wanna Run to You." It was far from professional quality as Christina had recorded it into a boom box in her family's living room — but it clearly showcased her multi-octave range. And it nailed the gig for her.

She's totally made head-wrap kerchiefs her fashion statement.

the jumpstart her career needed. It became a chart hit and Christina got to perform it on such TV shows as *CBS This Morning* and *The Donny & Marie Show*. Even cooler, the song got a Golden Globe Nomination for "Best Original Song in a Motion Picture," and Christina herself nabbed her first professional nod with an ALMA [American Latin Music Association] nomination for it.

Her good fortune didn't end there: The homemade tape

Fashion-forward: "I never put on what I don't feel comfortable with."

"I was ecstatic," she said. "They took a huge chance using an unknown like me." Christina totally identified with the lyrics. "The song's theme, the struggle to establish your identity, was something I could relate to as a teenage girl myself."

"Reflection" was just

"I'm a huge Lauryn Hill fan, for her sound, her style, and her talent."

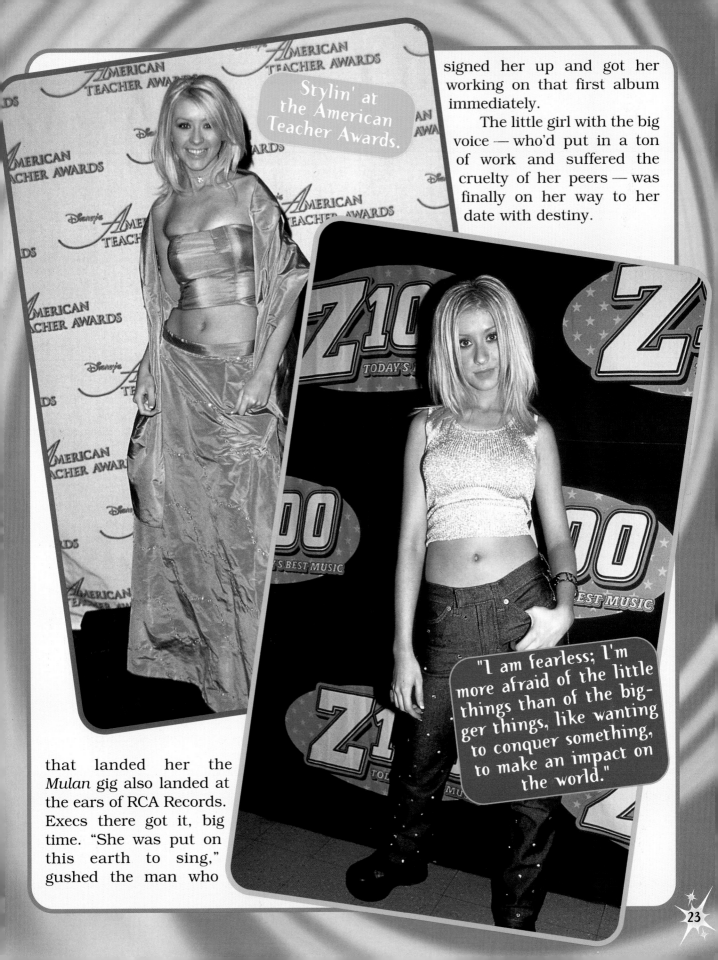

signed her up and got her working on that first album immediately.

The little girl with the big voice — who'd put in a ton of work and suffered the cruelty of her peers — was finally on her way to her date with destiny.

that landed her the *Mulan* gig also landed at the ears of RCA Records. Execs there got it, big time. "She was put on this earth to sing," gushed the man who

"I am fearless; I'm more afraid of the little things than of the bigger things, like wanting to conquer something, to make an impact on the world."

★ CHAPTER FOUR ★
FACTS AT YOUR FINGERTIPS ✦

"Music is always running through my mind."

"I'm living my dream."

Thumbnail Bio

Real Full Name: Christina Marie Aguilera
You Say It: Ag-we-**leh**-ra
Birthdate: December 18, 1980
Astro Sign: Sagittarius
Born In: Staten Island, New York
Lived In: Texas, New Jersey, Japan, Rochester, and Wexford, PA
Mom: Shelly Kearns
Dad: Fausto Aguilera
Stepdad: James Kearns
Sibs: Rachel — nicknamed, "Ro," is five years younger; stepsister Stephanie Kearns is 14; step-bro Casey Kearns is 17; half brother Robert Michael is four
Grandma: Delcie Fidler
Pets: A dog named Fozzie and a cat, Tiger

Stats 'N' Stuff

Height: 5′2″ — in heels
Hair: Blond
Eyes: Blue
School Stuff: Christina attended grade school and then Marshall Middle School in Wexford, PA. She left in eighth grade, and has been privately tutored ever since. She graduated high school in 1998.
School Subjects She Liked Best: English, science
Boyfriend: Rumors of romance with Carson Daly aside, Christina insists she's way too busy for commitment. "My schedule doesn't allow me to have a boyfriend," she told *TV Guide*. "My career is my boyfriend."
Date Destination: Christina thinks going to a museum on a date would

"[Sometimes] I think teens are overlooked and misunderstood."

Favorites

Junk Food: Wendy's bacon cheeseburgers, McDonald's Chicken McNuggets with mustard sauce, chili cheese fries

Pop Fizz: Coca-Cola

Actors: Tom Hanks, Drew Barrymore, Johnny Depp

Star Crush: Enrique Iglesias

Ex-Star Crush: Mark McGrath (Sugar Ray). "He's totally cute, but his whole presence is arrogance. Plus, I'm not diggin' the way he's looking now," she mentioned in *Rolling Stone*.

Star She Admires: Jennifer Lopez. "What draws me to her is that [like her] I feel proud of my Spanish roots. She's Hispanic and going out there — that's something I can relate to."

Being a *Star Search* runner-up did have some compensation at least. Her "lovely parting gift" was cash. She used her winnings to buy a portable sound system, which allowed her to perform in public parks around Wexford, PA.

be ultra-cool. "Museums are kind of romantic," she says, "they're so quiet and so like . . . artsy! I love being artsy."

Dream Date: "I do want to date a performer. It's important to me that I date someone who understands my schedule. I've had it with these guys who don't get it!"

Lives In: She splits her time between an apartment in New York City and her parents' home in Wexford, PA

Workout: Practicing those dance moves is all she needs

Car: None — she doesn't drive

Accessory She Can't Live Without: Red cellular phone

"Pop is actually my least favorite kind of music. I think it lacks real depth," she said to *YM* magazine.

Singers: Mariah Carey, Whitney Houston, Lauryn Hill, Brian McKnight

Band: Limp Bizkit

Blues Artists: Etta James, B.B. King

Backstreet Boy: AJ

Videos: Jay-Z's *Can I Get A*, cause everybody can bounce to it; TLC's *Unpretty*

Colors: Think pink — but also turquoise and purple

Sports: Baseball, volleyball

Words: "Cute, creative, artistic" — she uses 'em in sentences, much

Kicking Back: Hanging out with friends, going to the movies, taking bubble baths

Free Time: Shopping, dancing, sports

Book: *Reviving Ophelia* by Mary Pipher

Before the Grammys, *Billboard Online* voters gave her a whopping 70 percent of the Best New Artist vote. They were right!

Another Star She Admires: Sarah Michelle Gellar. "At the Teen Choice Awards, she made an effort to come back and compliment me on my performance, and I was like, 'Wow!'"

Star She'd Like to Duet With: Mariah Carey

Movies: *Mulan*, *The Little Mermaid*

Music: Blues, jazz, R & B

"A lot of people don't get to see my personal side, because right now my whole persona is that of being a pop star." [*New York Times*]

Fashion Forward: In the short time she's been in the spotlight, Christina has forged her fashion identity. Not that she always wears the same style, but she knows what she likes, and tends to stick with it. Like, belly-button baring halter tops, hip-hugging pants and skirts, and often, a colorful kerchief wrap on her head. "I wear a lot of long, side-slit skirts with cute tummy tops and funky shoes. Also, party-animal prints and form-fitting fabrics," is how she describes her look.

Favorite Designer: And what would a diva be without a favorite designer? Hers is Dolce & Gabbana. "The patterns are really cool. You can mix and match whatever."

Makeup That Matters: MAC

Confessions

Fondest Childhood Memory: "When I was seven, I was at my grandmother's at Christmas and I walked downstairs and there was a Barbie Kitchen waiting for me. I always wanted one, so I got real excited."

Childhood Toy: Barbie dolls, Barbie kitchen, Barbie house [trend alert!]

Embarrassing Admission: She still sleeps with the lights on, because she's afraid of the dark.

Christina on Christina: "I think that I'm eccentric. I'm a really deep thinker."

Christina on Christina, the sequel: "I'm a control freak, a perfectionist. And I have a problem being totally open and vulnerable, but once I get to know someone, that wall gets broken down."

Posing with LFO — one of the perks of being a pop star!

CHAPTER FIVE
WHAT THIS GIRL WANTS

Like any girl, Christina is complex. She has divergent opinions, styles, emotions, likes, dislikes, wants, needs, goals and especially, dreams. Only half the story of "what a girl wants" is told in her hit song — here's the rest.

In a guy

For an MTV special, Christina kicked it with three friends — including her younger sister, Rachel, or "Ro," — and dished about, among other topics, dudes. Christina doesn't have a boyfriend, but doesn't lack for opinions on what Mr. Right will be like. Here's her take the type of guy she goes for.

The Treat-You-Right Type: The most important quality in a guy, before anything else, is that he respects her.

The Rock-'n'-Roll Type: "I do go for the rock-'n'-roll type, but they have to lose the bad boy image when it's just the two of us. Bad boy in public is fine, but pussy cat at home is best."

all, a guy should be creative and artistic, maybe a handmade card with the box of chocolates."

The Real and Honest Type: Just being able to talk, to share, and to be open with each other is totally crucial.

What a Girl Doesn't Want

No Shy Guys: "The worst dates," she told *Smash Hits* magazine," are with guys too scared to talk to me. Back in my hometown I was sort of a local celebrity, so guys would be intimidated. . . it was kind of sad, 'cause all

She prefers winter to summer — and doesn't mind the rain at all.

The Confident Type: "A guy should come off as confident — that's what a girl wants!"

The Fun Type: "Funny, free-spirited, spontaneous, doesn't take himself too seriously."

The Romantic — and Creative — Type: On a holiday like Valentine's Day, for instance, Christina admits she's all over "the cheesy things," like chocolates, and flowers — but best of

"Being young does put more pressure on you if you want to be taken seriously as an artist. You have to be way sharper than anybody else, because people expect you to be this bubblegum airhead."

"Mariah Carey is my absolute hero — I'm dying to meet her."

guy to disrespect a girl — and abusive relationships are not to be tolerated," she and her friends agreed on TV.

No "too cool" types: "Trying to act too cool is the worst thing — a boy should relax and show me he likes me."

In a girlfriend

After all she's gone through with people being jealous of her, Christina knows better than most "what a girl wants" in a friend. "You learn the hard way who your friends are," Christina has noted. Now she looks for galpals who are loyal, who understand that she can't always be around, but will always be on the other end of the phone; who are supportive and not jealous; who listen; and who she can hang out with, shop with, giggle, and even cry with.

In a career

She's always had high career goals, and even though she's a mega-star, she still has ideals. "I want to succeed. I want to conquer something, make an impact on the world."

In her role models

"I look up to the greats, the experimental people, Madonna, Janet, who always have something new and creative

I wanted to do was have a laugh and get to know them."

No scrubs: It doesn't matter if a guy has no money, as long as he's trying, and isn't a slacker, is the point she made in her MTV special.

No dissers: "It is totally uncool for a

to offer the public. I hope with my career I'll be able to do the same."

To see the whole world

Although she's traveled a lot, there are two places she longs to see: Ireland, where her mom's family is from, and Ecuador, where her dad's kin are.

To not be misunderstood

Latin music is enjoying a huge boost in popularity now, thanks to Ricky Martin, Enrique Iglesias, Marc Anthony, and Jennifer Lopez. And now, the little blue-eyed blond with the Latin last name can also lay claim to a bit of that.

"Convenient timing" is what certain someones say — implying she's "cashing in" on the musical trend, even though, they point out, she doesn't even speak Spanish.

Okay, so here's the deal. Christina has never tried to come off as something she isn't. She has never lied about her roots, her background, or covered up her real upbringing. Her father comes from the South American country Ecuador — hence, biologically, she is half Latina.

Her parents were divorced when she was little, and admittedly, she's had little contact with her dad over the years. She speaks only "un poquito [a little bit]" of the language, and has to take lessons to record a planned album in Spanish. Here comes the "but."

She understands the majority of the language, she loves Ecuadoran food [mom cooks it], and most important, perhaps, she is totally proud of her Latina heritage and has made a commitment to learn more about it. So there!

What a girl believes

In Self-esteem: "Self-confidence is the key. You've gotta have it. People are going

Grammy goof: "I forgot to thank my sister and my brother [Robert, pictured here] — I hope they'll forgive me. I feel awful!"

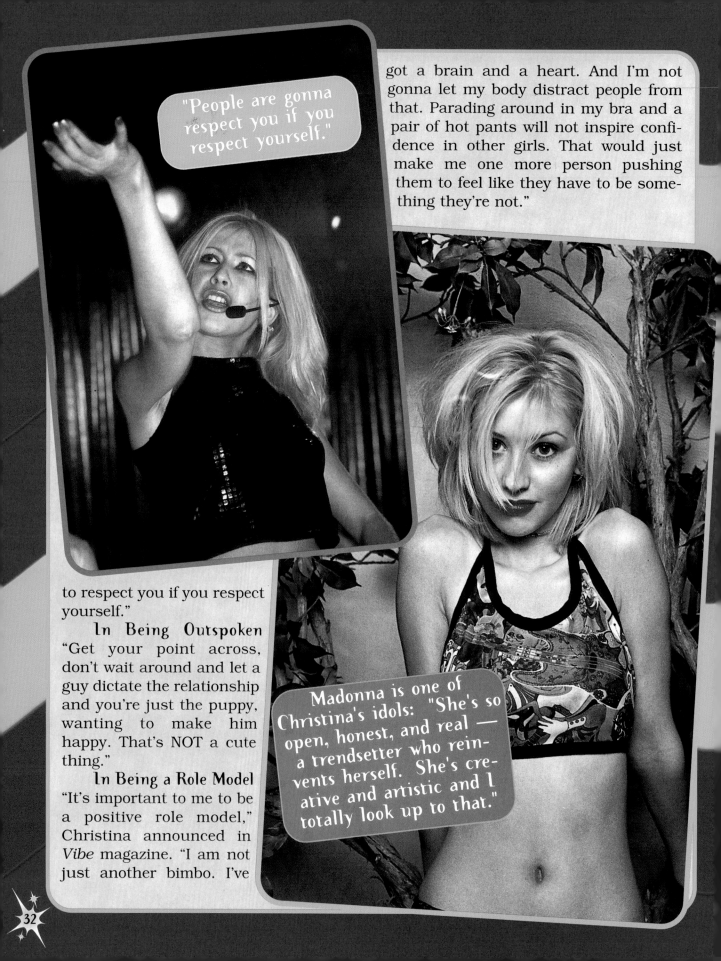

"People are gonna respect you if you respect yourself."

got a brain and a heart. And I'm not gonna let my body distract people from that. Parading around in my bra and a pair of hot pants will not inspire confidence in other girls. That would just make me one more person pushing them to feel like they have to be something they're not."

to respect you if you respect yourself."

In Being Outspoken
"Get your point across, don't wait around and let a guy dictate the relationship and you're just the puppy, wanting to make him happy. That's NOT a cute thing."

In Being a Role Model
"It's important to me to be a positive role model," Christina announced in *Vibe* magazine. "I am not just another bimbo. I've

Madonna is one of Christina's idols: "She's so open, honest, and real — a trendsetter who reinvents herself. She's creative and artistic and I totally look up to that."

Because Christina started performing at such a young age, it wasn't as if she had buds who "knew her when." She says, "I always envied people who had best friends they've known since they were little, because I've never had that. I'd have to keep picking up and moving."

CHRISTINA AGUILERA

CHAPTER SIX
THE MESSAGE IN THE MUSIC

"I Open My Mouth, and People Are Still Surprised By What Comes Out."

"Don't underestimate — big things come in small packages." Christina said that in an interview with *Entertainment Weekly* magazine, and she totally nailed it.

One listen is all it takes.

Christina, once tagged "the little girl with the big voice," demonstrates over and over again how true that still is. Even though she's only a tad over five feet tall, with a small-boned frame, her voice smoothly scales the octaves like practiced fingers gliding over a keyboard. Whether she's doing her uptempo, boogie down numbers, like "Genie in a Bottle," or "What a Girl Wants," or the power ballads "I Turn to You," "Reflection," or "We're a Miracle," her range is nothing short of amazing.

While she was recording her first album, producers had to hold her back. "A lot of times when I was recording, everyone was like, 'Okay, you need to tone it down.' But I like to do it my way!" On the ballad, "Obvious," she did get

she's famous for, but she has had a major say in choosing her tunes. Here's what goes into that decision: Will the song showcase her talents? What's it hit single potential? And, most important, what does it say to her listeners — will it connect with them and maybe inspire them?

Christina's all over the concept of a message in her music — a couple of to let loose with a gospel edge, and in "So Emotional," she got to take on an R & B side.

Christina's huge voice isn't used only to sing — there's a shout out message in her lyrics, and it reaches her audience as loudly and clearly as her songs. "It's Time That Music Makes Kids Feel Confident and Secure."

So far, Christina hasn't totally written any of the songs

"No matter how bad a situation is, it's your outlook that will either get you through, or mean that you fail..."

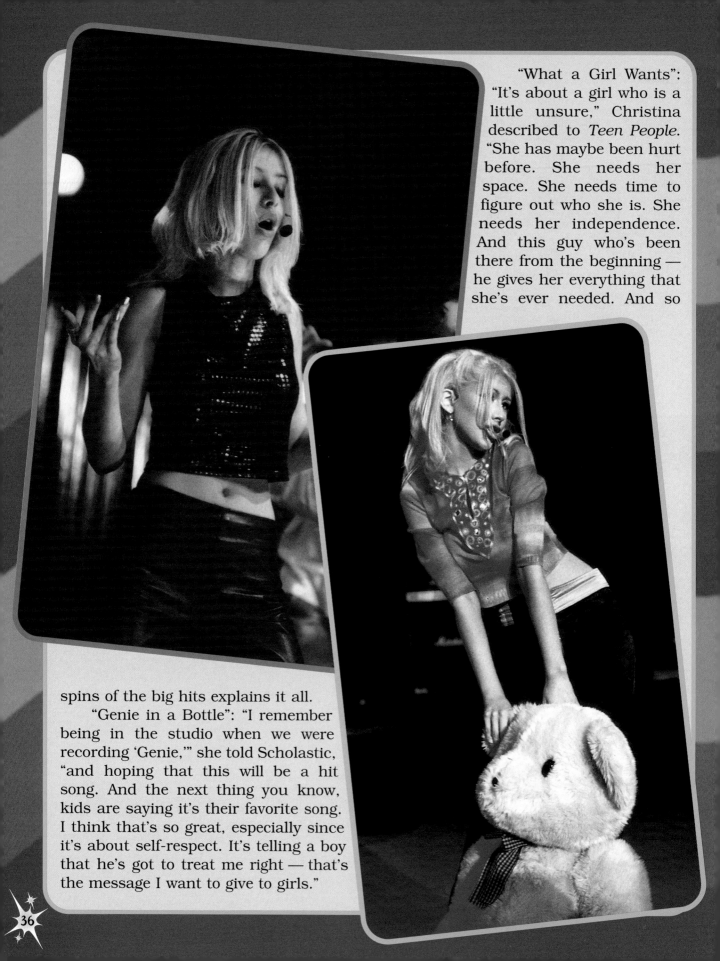

"What a Girl Wants": "It's about a girl who is a little unsure," Christina described to *Teen People*. "She has maybe been hurt before. She needs her space. She needs time to figure out who she is. She needs her independence. And this guy who's been there from the beginning — he gives her everything that she's ever needed. And so spins of the big hits explains it all.

"Genie in a Bottle": "I remember being in the studio when we were recording 'Genie,'" she told Scholastic, "and hoping that this will be a hit song. And the next thing you know, kids are saying it's their favorite song. I think that's so great, especially since it's about self-respect. It's telling a boy that he's got to treat me right — that's the message I want to give to girls."

when she's ready, he's right there for her to start a relationship."

"I Turn to You": Sure, it's a major love song, but it's really about two people being partners and supportive of each other, a "wind beneath my wings," friendship message. ("When I need a friend, you're always on my side")

"Reflection": "It's about finding yourself, and learning to love yourself. It's about positivity."

✴CHAPTER SEVEN✴
ALL THE RIGHT MOVES

"**I** *Really Love Being Onstage. It's Like Home to Me.*"

Sure, she's a hit-song machine, but it's not only about the grooves, for Christina Aguilera has the moves too. A concert experience is fun, not just for the audience, but for her as well. Up until last year, Christina's touring experience consisted mainly of lots of promotional and TV appearances. Only lately has she had the chance to strut her stuff in a full-blown tour. Here are some snaps and snippets from Christina onstage.

What's Best: "There's no other feeling in the world like getting onstage and connecting with so many people at once. It's amazing that I get the opportunity to do that on a daily basis, practically. Even if I'm tired, when I see the fans, my energy goes up immediately. This is what I live for: hearing them singing it back to me."

What's Cool: "On-stage, a lot of people think I am a lot stronger

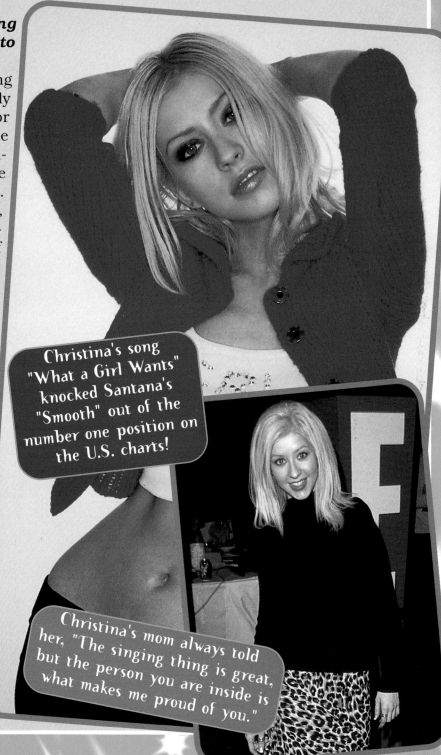

Christina's song "What a Girl Wants" knocked Santana's "Smooth" out of the number one position on the U.S. charts!

Christina's mom always told her, "The singing thing is great, but the person you are inside is what makes me proud of you."

"I was shocked when I won the Grammy for Best New Artist — my mind was blank!"

enough to me] lip sync. I think that's really unfair to those of us out there doing it for real. It's cool, but it's hard."

What's Self-Critical: "For a live show, I give it my all, and I usually do okay. Of course, I may say, 'Oh, I should have done this differently,' but there's always a next show."

What's Amazing: "I know it sounds cheesy, but when I hear everyone in the audience sing all the words along with me, I feel their energy, their love and their adoration. I hear that and I float on air."

What's Scary: "I began to sing and everyone tried to get closer to the stage. Then, there was some shoving and a fight broke out. I was afraid people were going to say 'Look, she's causing riots.' I didn't know if I should stop singing. I was a little scared, but I said, 'Could you guys stop fighting?' And they did!"

than I am because I exude so much strength sometimes — like when I come out into the audience."

What's Tough: "Dancing and singing is hard because you have to concentrate on more than one thing at once," she admitted to Scholastic. "You're trying to concentrate on the song, and on what your feet and arms are doing at the same time. So, it's a bit complicated, that's why a lot of people out there [frustratingly

What Was Rough: Of course, there are the run-of-the-mill spills onstage, microphones coming loose, or not working. Then there was the day everything went kerblooie. It was during a performance in New York City. She tripped over one of her dancers and did a total faceplant onstage. Then her pre-recorded music wouldn't work — she had to ditch two songs and did "Genie" a cappella.

CHAPTER EIGHT

PLANET CHRISTINA: ON FANS, FAMILY, FATIGUE, PHOTOGS — AND FUN!

She's got her own calendar and full-length video — it's called *The Genie Gets Her Wish.*

Touring, Traveling, TRL'ing: What a [Girl's] Life!

Life on planet Christina these days is a whirlwind of number one songs, recording, concert performances, photo shoots, interviews, meeting other stars, hairdressers, makeup artists, stylists . . . yeah, being pampered. How amazing is that? Mostly, majorly. Listen in as Christina shares her real feelings about . . .

FANS: "It gives me a feeling that's different from any other feeling in the world," is how she expressed it to the *New York Times.* "When I see all these people screaming and chanting and holding those signs that they made just for me, my eyes light up, my whole body just lifts, and I just feel in another state. I feel like I'm floating on air. It's the most incredible feeling, and I've always wanted it."

Reality check. Sometimes, the fan thing can be, well, not perfectly timed. "I had my first day off in forty days and I was planning on resting. But then I decided I wanted to be with my friends and have fun and go to the mall. I went without security and it was my first time back there and I just got mobbed. It's what I've always wanted — to be recognized, but at the same time it's exhausting and very weird. I went into one store and I had like thirty college and high school guys waiting outside the door for me."

And sometimes, it can be worse. Like the time Christina was set to do the autograph-signing thing at a Target department store, and total chaos erupted. Some people ended up waiting in line too long — and then, didn't get to meet her before she was whisked away. She felt terrible about it.

"It was overwhelming. I've never experienced anything like that before. I didn't know what to say. Everybody was climbing up the shelves. I am so sorry to anyone I might have left out. I tried to get to each and every one."

FRIENDS: No question, the friend thing has improved much from the bad old days when she had none. Slowly and carefully, Christina has been able to figure out who her real friends are — and how to hold onto them. In fact, two of her closest girl-buds were invited to be part of her MTV special.

But she hasn't forgotten the friend-sacrifices she made for her career. She told the *New York Post*, "There are definitely down sides to stardom. I missed

Christina's grateful that radio stations all over the world play her songs.

"The fans are incredible — they inspire me so much!"

to *Entertainment Weekly* magazine about a recent experience at the prom. Although she didn't physically attend high school (Christina was tutored, and earned her diploma), she did follow the curriculum of her local high school, and therefore was included in the prom. "I wasn't going to go," she related, "because I knew I would be treated a little different, but I finally called my friend and said, 'Let's just have fun with this.'" Fun was the one thing she didn't have. For starters, she'd asked her girlfriend to set her up with a blind date — that was fine, except she inadvertently hurt the feelings of another guy who'd planned on asking her. So she ended up with two dates for the prom. Once there, she was soundly ignored by the girls. "Only two girls came up to talk to me. Later I found out they were telling their boyfriends, 'If you talk to her, I'll kill you.'"

out on the whole going-to-school-thing with my friends, going to football games, going to proms. But if I was sitting in school right now, I'd probably be looking out the window, fantasizing about the life I'm living now."

And still, the jealousy thing manages to crop up every now and then. She talked

FAMILY: She's family-girl to the max, and tries really hard to include her 'rents and sibs in everything she does. They're often backstage at concerts, and in the wings during photo sessions and interviews. But that's only sometimes. Because of their own schedules, Christina's family is most often at home in Pennsylvania, while she's on the road. What of her biological dad? According to a *New York Times* article, Christina had (at the time the piece was written) "lost track" of her father.

FATIGUE: Living the life of a superstar means constant travel. After all, fans want to do the up-close-and-personal thing, and Christina really was born to entertain. And no question, when she travels it's first class and limos all the way. But, there is this, too, she reminded reporters: "I'm always so tired, that I'd say

> "It's important to be confident and believe in yourself no matter what!"

> In 1999, Christina was one of the celebrities involved in the Big Brother/Big Sister charity and served a turkey dinner to homeless kids — she did it as much for her fans as for the famished. "I feel like I've been given so much. I know a lot of kids see me as a role model. [Doing this] is a way I can inspire them more than just through my music."

the downside to all this is my schedule. It's so crazy, being in a different city every day. People tried to tell me, but nothing could have prepared me for this. There is just so much flying going on that sometimes, I have to ask, 'Where are we landing now?' It's really weird, and it can be draining."

She admitted to Scholastic, "I do have insecurities and everything is not perfect, you know

Publicity poses like this one are all part of the job.

guys all over you, and yeah, I do, but [I] don't have time to spend with anyone. Living out of two suitcases and flying all the time, you never get the sense of any place for very long, or get to feel at home."

PHOTOS: Being a coveted covergirl is cool, but when you're a star, pictures also get taken when you're far from prepared.

"The looks thing [feeling insecure about how you look] never goes away, and I think it gets worse as you get older. Sometimes you could be just rolling out of bed without your makeup and run into someone that wants a picture of you. Well, ten years later that picture still looks the same — yuck! So I'll always be self-conscious about how I look. But that's everyone."

This is her: "It's hard to be a teenager and be in this business. Your album is huge and these people twenty years your senior are seeing you as product. That can be scary. I just wanted to make music and all of a sudden it was all about this package — what your look is going to be. All these decisions are being made for you," she conceded to *Teen People*.

what I mean? It's hard to live this lifestyle, and to go out. It's extremely lonely too. People think, you must have all these

The Battle of the Pop Princesses

Naturally, Christina isn't the only teen superstar singer on the charts, but "unnaturally," she can't dodge the constant comparisons with others. Seems like every time she reads an article about herself, or appears on *TRL* even, she's "pitted" against other female singers who also happen to be under twenty-one.

There's Jessica Simpson ["Where You Are"], Mandy Moore ["Candy"], Hoku ["Another Dumb Blonde"] and Vitamin C ["Me, Myself & I"]. But mostly there's the girl Christina used to know as "Little Brit-Brit."

For some reason, the tabloids and the blabbermouths keep insisting there's this major rivalry between 'em. Sure, both are young, fair-haired former Mouseketeers; both have had mega-success in the past year, and both were even double Grammy nominees, for "Best Female Pop Vocal Performance," and "Best New Artist." But none of that makes for a battle. Not in the real world.

"I knew Britney as a kid from Louisiana. It's frustrating to be compared with her," she told the *New York Post*, "because we are two very different artists . . . we both dance and sing, but people have not yet had enough time to realize that there is a difference between us."

Britney agrees. ["This business is] about hard work and determination. Christina's got it, and she'll do really well."

Christina can't stop the comparisons, but she insists she doesn't support the websites where fans pit the two of them against one another. "Choosing sides is ridiculous," she says. "When Britney's album came out, I was the first one to buy it."

Britney Spears was also nominated for the "Best New Artist" Grammy, however, Christina expected Macy Gray to win.

CHAPTER NINE
DISCOGRAPHY & KUDOS

First Album:

Christina Aguilera, released August 24, 1999

Became #1: that week

Five times platinum [sold five million copies, as of 3/00]

Hit Singles:

"Reflection," — from the *Mulan* soundtrack, 1998

"Genie in a Bottle" — once heard, never purged; released 6/22/99

"What a Girl Wants"

"I Turn to You"

Soundtrack Gigs:

Mulan

Pokemon: The First Movie, "We're a Miracle"

Videography:

Full length video: *Christina Aguilera: The Genie Gets Her Wish* [BMG video]

WHOO-HOO!

Kudos for Christina: on the Music

Grammy Winner 2000 "Best New Artist"

"Reflection"
Nominated for a Golden Globe Award and an ALMA Award

"Genie in a Bottle"

Number one on the *Billboard* charts for five weeks and sold close to two million copies. Number one most-played video on MTV; heavy rotation on VH1

Christina was one of the stars on hand to announce the Grammy nominations — little did she know she'd soon win one!

We are the world: Number one in twenty countries

"What a Girl Wants"
Topped the charts for two weeks — knocked out by Savage Garden's "I Knew I Loved You"

Number one most played video on MTV for six straight weeks; heavy rotation at VH1

Number one most requested video on MTV's *TRL*

Christina Aguilera, the album, entered *Billboard*'s Top 200 Albums charts at number one — the same week Puff Daddy's newie, *Forever*, was predicted to take that slot.

Congrats on the Coverage
Cover girl: major mags have chosen her for their covers (*Teen People*, *YM*, *Latina*). Speaking of magazines, *Ladies' Home Journal* voted her one of the "most fascinating women of 1999," and she appeared in their TV special, which aired 1/2/00.

Big Time Appearances
MTV's New Year's Eve Millennium Bash in Times Square.

The 2000 Super Bowl half-time game: she dueted with Enrique Iglesias.

Fascinating Factoid: According to *Billboard* magazine, Christina became the first RCA artist in the rock era to have two number one hits as a solo female artist.

Christina's official website features a section called "The Rumor Mill" — where she debunks the stuff that's not true.

WEBGIRL
The official clicks are:
www.peeps.com/christina
www.Christina-A.com

SNAILMAIL
The Christina Aguilera Fan Club
244 Madison Ave., Suite 314
New York, NY 10016

CHAPTER TEN
S'UP! WHAT'S NEXT ON CHRISTINA'S CALENDAR

Think she's got a lot on her plate already? That's nothing compared to the plans she's got for the coming year. They include . . .

A CHRISTMAS ALBUM: Christina will mix standards with new holiday songs.

A SPANISH ALBUM: "*Genio Atrapado*" is the Spanish version of "Genie in a Bottle." It's the first track on a planned Spanish-language album, which will also include a duet with Enrique Iglesias.

COMPOSING SONGS: "I really like to write, and I'm really interested in co-writing songs on my next album," Christina has said.

PRODUCING AN ALBUM: "I think there should be more female producers like Lauryn Hill," is her quote about that concept.

ACTING: "I'm so interested in acting," she told the *New York Daily News*. "I am going to be looking for a role with some real acting, rather than just guest-performing as myself. But singing is my first love."

ON TV: Christina is part of the Disney Channel's Two Hour Tour, an on-the-road-type documentary. She was filmed doing concerts in Pittsburgh. The special also includes concerts by the Moffatts [sponsored by Scholastic!!] and 98°.

4-A-CAUSE GIRL: Perhaps the goal that's closest to her heart is this: "I want to use my popularity to take up the cause of battered children and women. That's what I meant when I said I wanted to make an impact on the world."

Just follow your heart, know what you want — and go for it!